Introdu

After the success of my first book, Teddy Bears, I have been inspired to move onto my next exciting project. Making Sugar Cats for Cakes has new ideas and projects for a range of hobbies and celebrations. My daughter, Amy, came up with all the titles for the cakes and then I had the time consuming job of designing them! There are ideas for men's cakes – which always seem to challenge me – and Valentine's Day, Christening, Halloween and Christmas projects are all included. I have aimed to appeal to beginners and advanced sugarcrafters alike – the basic designs can be adapted to suit the occasion or you can cut out some of the work to simplify the design. To make each project as easy as possible, I have included all the step-by-step stage work.

I hope you enjoy this handy little book and find inspiration for your own projects.

Susan

Susan Griffiths

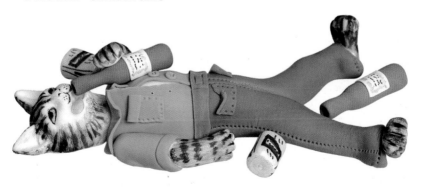

To my dear Mother and daughters, Amy and Abbie, for having
to put up with my stresses whilst working on this book!

Thanks to Beverley, Robert, Jenny, Sarah, Clare and Zena for all their hard
work behind the scenes.

Also thank you to Alister for his fabulous photography.

First published in September 2005 by B. Dutton Publishing Limited, Alfred House,
Hones Business Park, Farnham, Surrey, GU9 8BB.

Copyright: Susan Griffiths 2005

ISBN: 1-905113-01-3

Publisher: Beverley Dutton

Editor: Jenny Stewart

Design: Sarah Richardson

Editorial Assistant: Clare Porter

Design Assistant: Zena Manicom

Photography: Alister Thorpe

Printed in Spain

Contents

Projects:

Recipes

All the cakes in this book can be rich fruit cake or a sponge cake such as Madeira. Use the chart opposite as a guide to the quantity of ingredients you will require and cooking times.

Basic Fruit Cake Recipe

Ingredients

450g/1lb mixed fruit

40g/1½oz glacé cherries, chopped

110g/4oz plain flour

1.5ml/¼tsp cinnamon

2.5ml/½tsp grated nutmeg

110g/4oz butter

110g/4oz dark brown soft sugar

2 eggs

Grated rind of ½ orange and ½ lemon

5ml/1tsp black treacle

40g/1½oz chopped almonds

30ml/2tbsp brandy

Preparation

Soak the fruit in the brandy overnight before making the cake.

Method

1. Cream the butter and sugar until light and fluffy. Gradually add the eggs. Fold in the flour and spices. Stir in the fruit, nuts, treacle and citrus fruits. Spoon into prepared tins, spread evenly and depress the centre slightly.

2. Cook in a preheated oven at 140°C/275°F/Gas Mark 1.

3. When cooked, leave in the tin to cool. To store, double wrap in greaseproof paper then in foil.

Basic Madeira Cake Recipe

Ingredients

110g/4oz butter or sunflower margarine

110g/4oz caster sugar

110g/4oz self-raising flour

2 eggs

Method

1. Place all the ingredients into a mixer and beat well. If you require the cake to be firmer than usual, e.g. for a cutting cake, add a little more flour. Place in a prepared tin.

2. Cook at 180°C/350°F/Gas Mark 4. For larger cakes, lower the heat and increase cooking time.

3. Upturn the baked cake onto a sugared piece of greaseproof paper and cover with a clean tea towel until cooled.

Ingredient Quantities and Cooking Times

This chart shows all the cake sizes used in the projects in this book, the quantity of ingredients required for each (based on the recipes opposite) and how long the cake should be baked for.

Cake shape	Cake tin size (width x depth)	Multiple of cake recipe	Cooking time: FRUIT	Cooking time: MADEIRA
Round	20.5 x 7.5cm/8 x 3″	2	4 – 4$\frac{1}{2}$ hrs	35 – 40 mins
Square	15 x 5cm/6 x 2$\frac{1}{2}$″	1$\frac{1}{2}$	3$\frac{1}{2}$ – 4 hrs	30 – 35 mins
Square	20.5 x 7.5cm/8 x 3″	2$\frac{1}{2}$	4$\frac{1}{4}$ – 4$\frac{3}{4}$ hrs	40 – 45 mins
Oval	20.5 x 15 x 7.5cm/8 x 6 x 3″	1$\frac{1}{2}$	3 - 3$\frac{1}{2}$ hrs	30 – 35 mins
Hexagon	20.5 x 7.5cm/8 x 3″	2	4 – 4$\frac{1}{2}$ hrs	35 – 40 mins
Hexagon	30.5 x 10cm/12 x 4″	5	6 – 6$\frac{1}{2}$ hrs	N/A*
Heart	20.5 x 7.5cm/8 x 3″	2$\frac{1}{2}$	3$\frac{1}{2}$ – 4 hrs	40 – 45 mins

*This size not suitable for sponge mixes.
Please note that the cooking temperature and time may vary depending on your oven.

Cake Covering Quantities

These are the amounts of marzipan and sugarpaste you will need for the sizes of cake in this book.

Cake shape	Cake size	Marzipan/sugarpaste required to cover cake
Round	20.5cm/8″	680g/1$\frac{1}{2}$lb
Square	15cm/6″	680g/1$\frac{1}{2}$lb
Square	20.5cm/8″	910g/2lb
Oval	20.5 x 15cm/8 x 6″	455g/1lb
Hexagon	20.5cm/8″	680g/1$\frac{1}{2}$lb
Hexagon	30.5cm/12″	1590g/3$\frac{1}{2}$lb
Heart	20.5cm/8″	910g/2lb

Materials

Marzipan

Squires Kitchen make a smooth and easy-to-use marzipan, so I find no need to make my own. Whether you choose to buy or make your own marzipan, always ensure it is of high quality, i.e. has a smooth texture and an almond content of at least 30%.

Sugarpaste

It is easiest to use a ready-made sugarpaste for cake covering. This is available in a range of colours, but if you wish to colour white sugarpaste, use a cocktail stick to apply paste food colour into a small piece of paste. Knead well, then blend this coloured piece into the remaining sugarpaste. It is always wise to colour more sugarpaste than required as it can be tricky to match the colour again should you need more.

SK Mexican Modelling Paste (MMP)

Throughout the book, MMP has been used for all the cats and modelling.

SK White MMP can be coloured using the range of SK QFC Paste Food Colours, as with sugarpaste.

SK Sugar Florist Paste (SFP)

SFP is a stronger paste than MMP, which makes it ideal for making sugar flowers and leaves, tiny bows and other delicate items. It is also used on some of the girls' dresses that require a very fine paste rolled out thinly.

SK Pastillage

SK Pastillage is a powder mix that is made up by adding water. This is the strongest paste and dries hard. I have used this in the Christmas design for making the plates. Pastillage work can be made well in advance and stored in a non-airtight container (e.g. a cake box) until required.

Royal icing

Squires Kitchen manufacture a high quality royal icing mix which simply requires the addition of water. Make up following the instructions on the packet. However, if you wish to make your own royal icing, the basic recipe is as follows:

1. Pour 75ml/5 tablespoons of water into a clean electric mixing bowl and add 15ml/1 tablespoon dried egg albumen (fortified). Blend until smooth.

2. Weigh out 455g/1lb icing sugar. Set the mixer to a slow speed and gradually mix in approximately half of the icing sugar until the consistency is similar to unwhipped cream.

3. Gradually add the remaining sugar and mix until the icing is smooth and glossy. (You may need slightly more or less icing sugar to achieve the correct consistency.)

Edible food colours

These are available in the following forms:

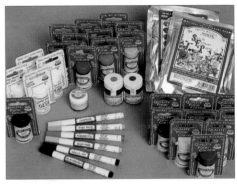

SK Quality Food Colour (QFC) Pastes: use for colouring sugarpaste, MMP, SFP and royal icing. Paste colours do not alter the consistency of the paste/icing as much as liquid colours.

SK Quality Food Colour (QFC) Liquids: can be used to colour royal icing and are ideal for painting fine details such as eyes and noses.

SK Quality Food Colour (QFC) Dusts: use to highlight cheeks, ears, etc. Dust colours are ideal for painting when blended with clear alcohol as the colour dries quickly.

SK Quality Food Colour (QFC) Lustre Dusts (Gold, Pearl and Silver): brush onto cakes to add a sheen. Ideal for bridal outfits and snowy scenes. Can be mixed with a little clear alcohol, confectioners' glaze or cooled, boiled water to create a metallic paint.

SK Hi Strength Paste Food Colours: the Black and Red colours in this range have been used on items such as the boxing gloves on 'Cat Fight', where a particularly strong colour is needed.

SK Magic Sparkle Dust: can be brushed over paste to give a glittery, shimmering effect.

SK Food Pens: the plain-nibbed pens are useful for writing on small items such as the cards on 'Cat with 9 Lives', where painting could be tricky.

SK QFC Edible Glue

A clear glue which is ideal for securing sugar pieces together.

White vegetable fat

Rubbing a little white vegetable fat onto a non-stick board before rolling out modelling paste or flower paste will help to prevent the paste from sticking to the board. It also helps to keep colours vibrant.

Cornflour

Dust onto a non-stick board before rolling out flower paste for frilling and making flowers and leaves. To make a cornflour duster, put some cornflour on a small piece of fine muslin and tie up the corners with an elastic band.

Clear alcohol

A clear spirit, such as gin or vodka, is ideal for diluting dust food colours to make a quick-drying paint.

Equipment

Essential Equipment

Blade and shell tool (PME)

Bone tool (PME)

Cake smoothers

Cat head moulds: large, medium and small (SK)

CelSticks: large and small (CC)

Cocktail sticks

Cutting wheel (PME)

Dresden/stitching tool (PME)

Dusting brush (SK)

Greaseproof piping bags: large and small

Kitchen towel

Nutmeg grater

Paint palette (or saucer)

Paintbrushes: sizes 00 and 4 (SK)

Palette knife

Pastry brush

Piping bags

Piping nozzle: no. 1

Polythene rolling-out board

Polythene rolling pins: large and small

Scalpel (PME)

Small, sharp knife

Spaghetti, raw

Sponge

Sugar shaker (for icing sugar)

Before you start making sugar cats, you will need some basic tools and equipment. The items listed here are needed for most, if not all, the projects in this book, so it is worth investing in these items if you do not already have them. As you work through each project, you will find that there are other items listed at the beginning. These are more specialised items which are only needed for some of the projects. I have given abbreviations of the manufacturers' names beside each item (e.g. SK = Squires Kitchen) and a list of stockists and manufacturers is given on the inside back cover.

Basic Techniques

Covering a Cake Board (Drum)

1. Knead the sugarpaste well and roll out thinly on a non-stick board dusted with icing sugar.

2. Lay the paste over the cake board and roll again. Trim away the excess paste from the board edge using a sharp knife.

3. Using a pastry brush, dampen the top surface of the board around the edge with a little cooled, boiled water, lifting the paste as you do so, to stick the paste to the board.

4. Re-roll the paste and trim the edges again. Cut out the paste from the centre, the same shape as the cake but a little smaller.

Covering a Fruit Cake with Marzipan

1. Brush the edge of the cake top with apricot glaze and position a roll of marzipan around the edge. Flatten with a palette knife.

2. Fill in any holes on the cake surface with small pieces of marzipan.

3. Upturn the cake onto a work board sprinkled with icing sugar. Brush the top and sides of the cake with apricot glaze, roll out the required amount of marzipan and lay over the cake. Use the palm of your hand to push the marzipan against the cake, then carefully trim to size. Make sure there are no creases along the bottom edge of the cake.

4. Trim away any excess paste at the bottom of the cake.

5. Smooth the marzipan on the top and sides with a pair of cake smoothers.

Covering a Fruit Cake with Sugarpaste

1. Brush a little brandy or clear spirit (e.g. gin or vodka) onto the surface of the marzipanned cake.

2. Take the amount of sugarpaste required and knead well until pliable. Roll out on a non-stick board dusted with icing sugar,

ensuring the area of the paste will cover the top and sides of the cake.

3. Lay the paste over the prepared cake. Carefully smooth down the sides using the palm of your hand. Trim and finish with smoothers, in the same way as for the marzipan.

4. Using a smoother, push the cake to the board edge, onto your hand and place on a covered cake drum.

Covering a Madeira Cake

1. Cut the cake in half horizontally and sandwich with buttercream or a filling of your choice. Place on a non-stick board and spread a thin, even layer of buttercream over the top and sides of the cake.

2. Cover with sugarpaste using the method above and place onto a prepared cake drum.

I always like to trim the board edge with 15mm ribbon in a colour that will complement the cake. Use a non-toxic glue stick to attach the ribbon and make sure the join is at the back.

How to Make a
Basic Cat

The cats are made in SK White Mexican Modelling Paste. They are then dressed, left to dry and then painted with the SK QFC range of edible food dusts.

Sizes

There are three sizes of SK Great Impressions Cat Head Moulds available: large, medium and small. The total amount of paste needed for each cat (including body, limbs and tail) is as follows:

Large: 85g/3oz

Medium: 55g/2oz

Small: 30g/1oz

Use the sizing guide at the front of the book to proportion the paste, or weigh out the paste as you go along following the instructions for each cat.

The general principles for making the head, body, arms, legs and tail are the same for all sizes of cat.

The instructions for making a large cat head (opposite) can be adapted for medium and small cats. Remember that you will need to make the head in advance to allow time for the paste to firm before painting.

10

Large Cat Head

1. Roll 15g of MMP into a ball and then into a cone.

2. Insert the point of the cone into the nose area of the cat head mould. Push the paste well into the mould and round off the back of the head. Texture the paste on the back of the head with a Dresden tool to create a fur effect.

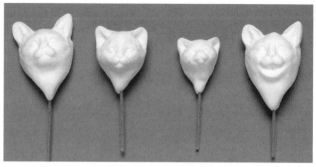

3. Ease the head out of the mould by gently pulling the paste out from the neck end. Try not to bend the mould as this will distort the head. Push a piece of raw spaghetti (approximately 5cm/2″ long) halfway into the neck. Place in a polystyrene block to firm.

If you find that the MMP is sticking to the mould, rub a little white vegetable fat in the palm of your hand when making the cone for the head. This will make the surface of the paste slightly greasy and easier to remove from the mould.

4. Repeat this method until you have enough heads for the project. It is always a good idea to have spares as well!

5. Allow to dry. Leaving the heads in a warm, dry place such as an airing cupboard will speed up the drying process.

Painting a Cat Head

It is always easier to paint the head before the cat is put together. Dust food colours give a subtle colour and liquid food colours will dry completely, so are ideal for this purpose. Paste colours, however, do not always dry out completely so are best avoided.

1. Dust the cheeks, ears and nose with SK Pink QFC Dust. (Always dab off any excess dust onto kitchen towel first and use sparingly.)

2. Dust the eyes with SK Blue or Dark Green QFC Dust.

3. Using a fine no. 00 paintbrush, paint the pupils and around the eyes with SK Black QFC Liquid. To prevent the paint from running down the face, blot any excess liquid from the paintbrush onto kitchen towel beforehand.

4. Paint a line along the top of the mouth. Paint the nose and add little dots around the nose area.

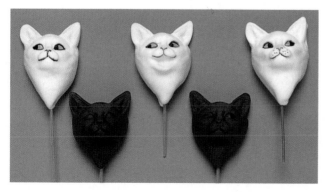

Basic Large Cat Body and Limbs

The principles for making the body and limbs are also the same for any cat. However, when you are dressing the cats, you will notice that the methods vary and you may not need to make the entire basic cat first. (For example, the 'Green-Fingered Cats' have only part of their body showing and the 'Boozy Cats' are wearing trousers.)

1. Roll 25g (1oz) of MMP into a ball and then into a cone shape. Flatten the top (point) and push in the sides where the arms and legs will go. Mark all over with the Dresden tool to achieve a fur effect. Indent the top with a large CelStick.

2. To make the legs, roll 15g (½oz) of MMP into a ball and cut in half. Roll each half into a cylinder shape. Using your little finger, roll over the bottom end of each leg to form the paws. Flatten slightly and make three indents with the blade tool. Texture the legs with the Dresden tool. Secure to the body with SK Edible Glue.

3. To make the arms (front legs), repeat the method as for the legs using the same quantity of paste. Position at the shoulders of the body, placing the front paws in between the legs.

4. To make the tail, roll 10g (⅓oz) of MMP into a ball and then into a long cylinder, tapering at one end. Attach to the body and twist into position.

When making the figures, it is easier to work on a small cake card as this can be moved around easily and can be put to one side for drying. The painting is also easier and you will not risk marking the cake. If you are making a cat in a sitting position, place an object such as a jam jar behind it for support whilst drying. Once firm, the figure can be placed in position on the cake.

The cats can be dressed for any occasion and can be adapted from the ideas I have given in this book. In each project, I have listed all the specialist equipment required and explained how to decorate each cake. This is followed by full instructions on how to dress the cats for that special occasion.

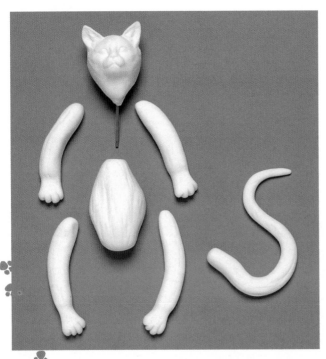

Cat with 9 Lives

Materials

15cm/6" square cake

800g/1³/₄lb white sugarpaste

75g/2¹/₂oz SK Mexican Modelling Paste (MMP): White

100g/3¹/₂oz SK Sugar Florist Paste (SFP): White

SK QFC Dusts: Blue, Brown, Green, Orange and Pink

SK QFC Liquid: Black

SK QFC Pastes: Blue, Brown, Green and Yellow

SK Food Pens: Baby Blue, Baby Pink and Daffodil

Equipment

23cm/9" square cake drum

Script alphabet cutter set: upper case (FMM)

Strip cutter: 7mm (JC)

Method

1. Colour the sugarpaste with Blue QFC Paste to a pale blue shade. Cover the board and cake. Position the cake centrally on the board. Leave to firm.

2. Roll out some White SFP thinly and cut strips with the 7mm strip cutter. Place in twirls around the base board to represent bandages. Attach with edible glue.

3. Cut out several tiny greetings cards from White SFP and fold three of them flat for the top of the cake. When they have dried, draw on designs with the edible food pens.

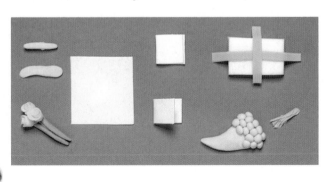

13

4. Colour tiny amounts of MMP yellow, green and brown using the QFC pastes. Make the rolled rose buds and grapes. Wrap the roses in a square of thinly rolled SFP to form a bouquet. Model a present and position on the cake.

5. Make the tabby cat. To make the bandages, cut out strips from White SFP with the 7mm strip cutter. Wrap around the tail, one leg, the head and neck. Place the cat in position on the cake.

6. Cut out the lettering from White SFP and glue in front of the cat on the top of the cake.

'Get Well Soon' Tabby Cat

1. Make a medium cat head from White MMP. Leave to firm.

2. Paint the face on the cat, giving him blue eyes. Leave the face to dry.

3. Model the body from White MMP. Make the back legs and attach to the body, bending them out into a splayed position. Make the arms (front legs) and place in-between the back legs.

4. Attach the head with edible glue and finally add a tail. Leave the whole figure to dry before painting.

Painting the Cat

1. To make a pale tabby colour, mix some Orange and Brown QFC Dusts with clear alcohol in a paint palette. Paint a wash over the cat using a no. 4 paintbrush, dabbing off any excess paint onto kitchen towel. Leave the chest and face area white. Leave to dry before painting the stripes.

2. Using the same colours as before, mix up a stronger brown colour. Paint in the stripes on the arms and legs using a no. 00 paintbrush and downward strokes.

3. Paint around the face, moving the brush strokes inwards towards the nose. Paint the back of the head and in-between the toes. Leave to dry.

The Love Boat

Materials

20.5cm/8" heart-shaped cake

910g/2lb white sugarpaste

300g/10oz SK Mexican Modelling Paste (MMP): White

200g/7oz SK Pastillage

75g/2½oz SK Sugar Florist Paste (SFP): White

SK QFC Dusts: Black, Blue, Brown, Dark Green and Pink

SK QFC Liquid: Black

SK QFC Pastes: Blue, Brown and Green

SK Hi Strength Paste Food Colour: Red

Royal icing

An orange (or similar round object)

Equipment

28cm/11" heart-shaped cake drum

Bow cutter: small (JC)

Button tools (HP)

Clingfilm

Heart cutter: small (FMM)

White ribbon: 2.5cm/1" width

Method

1. Colour the white sugarpaste with Blue QFC Paste. Cover the board and cake with the blue sugarpaste. Leave to firm and then place the cake centrally on the board.

2. Attach the white ribbon to the base of the cake.

Boat

1. Make up the pastillage and place in a food-grade polythene bag.

2. Blend 75g of White MMP with 75g of the pastillage. Colour the paste with Brown QFC Paste. Roll out the paste on a polythene board dusted with cornflour to a thickness of 5mm.

3. Cut out the boat using the template (see page 48).

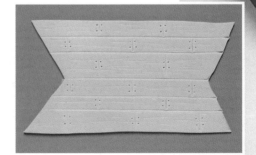

4. Mark the wood effect with a Dresden tool. Bend up and glue the ends together to form the boat shape. Flatten out the base. Place on a cake card to dry.

5. Paint a wash over the boat using Brown QFC Dust diluted with clear alcohol. When dry, place the boat in position on the cake.

6. Swirl royal icing on the top surface of the cake around the boat.

Parasol

1. Wrap a piece of clingfilm around an orange; this will be used as a former for the parasol.

2. Roll out the pastillage on a polythene board dusted with cornflour. Cut out the parasol using the template (see page 48). Roll a cutting wheel very gently over the paste to create the pattern, taking care not to cut right through the paste.

3. Roll a tiny ball of paste and glue it in the centre using edible glue.

4. Place the parasol over the orange to dry. When the top is dry, carefully remove the parasol and place it upside-down on a piece of foam to allow the underside to dry.

5. For the handle, roll a length of pastillage, using a smoother to create an even roll. Cut to size and allow to dry on a piece of foam. If you have spare paste, it is a good idea to make extra pieces to allow for breakages.

Hearts and Roses

1. Colour 25g of White SFP deep red using Hi Strength Red Paste Food Colour.

2. Roll out the red paste and cut out enough hearts for the umbrella and sides of the cake.

3. Make tiny rolled rose buds using the stage work as a guide. Colour a tiny amount of paste green and make the stems for the roses.

4. Attach the hearts to the white ribbon with tiny dots of royal icing. Place more hearts around the edge of the parasol, securing with royal icing.

5. Position three roses, complete with stems, on the top of the cake.

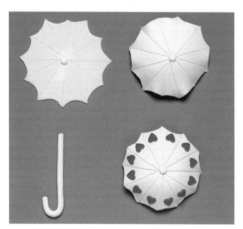

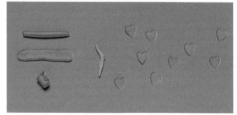

To Finish

Make the Love Cats (see opposite) and place them in the boat. Secure the parasol in the boat with a little royal icing.

Love Cats

Prepare two large size heads, giving the boy green eyes and the girl blue. Paint the pupils so they are looking at each other. Paint eyelashes on the girl.

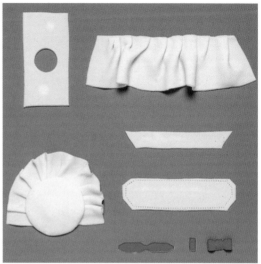

Girl

1. Model the large body and legs of the girl from White MMP, placing her in a sitting position.

2. Cut out the bodice from White MMP using the template (see page 48) and glue in place.

3. Cut out the skirt from the template. Pleat along the top edge, flatten with a large CelStick and re-cut. Attach to the body with the join at the back.

4. Cut out more hearts from the red SFP and attach to the skirt with edible glue whilst the paste is still soft.

5. At this stage, place the cat in the boat. Bend her legs into position with her foot resting on the front of the boat. Make the arms in the usual way and bend into position.

6. Paint the cat as a grey tabby using diluted Black QFC Dust and allow to dry.

7. For the brim of the hat, cut a strip of White MMP measuring 22cm x 2.5cm and pleat. Roll a ball of paste for the crown of the hat and flatten out with your fingers. Glue the brim and crown onto the cat's head and bend the brim into position.

Boy

1. Make a large body and legs from White MMP. Secure the legs to the body, bending one foot over the other.

2. Roll out a piece of White MMP and cut out the collar using the template (see page 48). Attach to the body with edible glue.

3. Cut out the waistcoat from White MMP using the template. Run the stitching wheel around the edge. Attach to the body, joining at the front.

4. Make the arms and secure in place. Indent his right paw with a blade tool and glue in a rose and stalk.

5. Attach the head, then place the cat in the boat, resting one arm on the boat and securing the other arm touching the girl's arm. Make a tail and drape it over the edge of the boat. Paint the boy in the same way as the girl.

6. Cut out a red bow from the coloured SFP and make the buttons for the waistcoat. Secure in place with edible glue.

Pusses in Boots

Materials

20.5 x 15cm/8 x 6" oval cake

910g/2lb white sugarpaste

170g/6oz SK Mexican
Modelling Paste (MMP): White

100g/3½oz SK Sugar Florist
Paste (SFP): White

SK QFC Dusts: Black, Brown,
Green, Orange and Pink

SK QFC Liquid: Brown

SK QFC Pastes: Black, Dark
Green, Green and Yellow

SK Pollen-Style Dust Food
Colour: Russet

Royal icing

Equipment

28 x 23cm/11 x 9" oval cake
drum

Blossom plunger cutter set
(FMM)

Metal sieve

Short friller tool (JC)

Six-petal flower cutter: small
(OP)

Method

1. Set aside 50g of the white sugarpaste for the pebbles. Colour the remaining white sugarpaste with Green QFC Paste and cover the board and then the cake. Position the cake centrally on the board.

2. Weigh out 75g of sugarpaste trimmings left over from covering the cake and board. Colour the paste a deeper green and push the paste through a metal sieve to create grass. Arrange the grass around the base of the cake and in clumps on the top of the cake.

3. Add a small amount of Black QFC Paste to the reserved white sugarpaste. Roll into pebble shapes and place around the cake.

4. Roll out some White SFP and cut out several blossoms using the cutter. Plunge them onto a piece of sponge and leave to firm. Place the

blossoms around the cake on the grass, securing with royal icing. Pipe dots of yellow royal icing in the centres.

5. Colour some SFP yellow for the daffodils. Roll out and cut at least eight six-petal flowers. Vein each flower with the friller tool, place on a piece of sponge and cup by pushing a bone tool into the centre.

6. Mould several tiny cones of paste and open up the centre of each with the short friller tool. Place a cone into each flower and secure with edible glue. Leave to firm. Dust the centres with Orange QFC Dust.

7. Colour a small amount of MMP with Dark Green QFC Paste to make the stems for the daffodils. Mould several tapered cones and attach to the sides of the cake. Mark with a Dresden tool.

8. Attach the daffodils to the stalks with royal icing. Reserve one flower and stem for the cat's paw.

9. Colour some royal icing dark green and stipple around the cake and board.

Wellington Boots

1. Blend 50g of White MMP with 50g of White SFP and colour dark green.

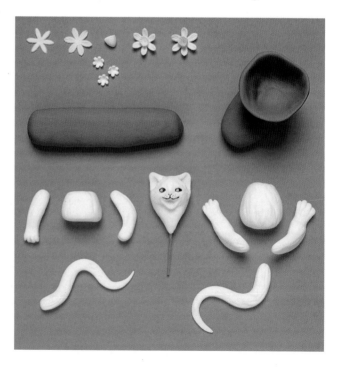

2. Divide the coloured paste in half and roll each piece into a ball and then into a cylinder. Bend up the foot and open up the other end using a small rolling pin. Open the top of the boot wider using your thumb and finger, making sure there is enough room for the cat to sit inside the top. Mark the sole and the heel. Repeat to make the second boot and leave to firm.

3. Position on the cake, laying one boot on its side.

To Finish

1. Make the Green-Fingered Cats and place in position on the cake.

2. Colour some royal icing brown and pipe some into the second boot around the back of the cat. Dab some icing on the ground in front of the boot.

3. Sprinkle Russet Pollen Dust onto the wet icing to represent soil.

4. Brush Brown QFC Dust onto the first cat's paws, nose and tail and onto the toes of the boots.

5. Place a daffodil and stem in the paw of the cat, securing with royal icing.

Green-Fingered Cats

1. Make only one medium-sized cat head. Open up the mouth with a Dresden tool and leave to firm before painting.

2. Model just the top part of the body with 5g of White MMP. Texture and glue the body into the Wellington boot. Secure the head to the body.

3. Using 5g of MMP, mould the arms and position them hanging over the front of the boot.

4. Make a tail and position it over the back of the upright boot, draping it over the second boot.

5. Model the back end only of the second cat with 10g of White MMP. Position in the second boot. Mould the back legs and tail from 10g of MMP and secure in place.

Painting the Cats

Paint both the cats as ginger tabbies (see 'Get Well Soon' Tabby Cat on page 14). Give the one in the upright boot green eyes and leave to dry.

Cat's Cradle

Materials

20.5 x 15cm/8 x 6" oval cake

910g/2lb white sugarpaste

300g/10oz SK Mexican
Modelling Paste (MMP): White

SK QFC Dusts: Dark Green and
Pink

SK QFC Liquid: Black

SK QFC Lustre Dust: Pearl

SK QFC Pastes: Brown, Green,
Orange, Pink and Yellow

SK Pastel Dust Food Colours:
Pastel Pink, Soft Green, Soft
Lemon and Wedgwood Blue

SK Food Pens: Baby Blue, Baby
Pink and Daffodil

Equipment

28 x 23cm/11 x 9" oval cake
drum

Basket embosser (PC)

Bow cutter: medium (JC)

Frilling tool (JC)

Garrett frill cutter (OP)

Pink ribbon

Quilting embosser (PC)

Method

1. Colour the sugarpaste with Pink QFC Paste and cover the board and cake. Place the cake centrally on the board.

2. Secure a length of thin pink ribbon around the base of the cake with royal icing, ensuring the join is at the back.

3. To make the blanket on the board, roll out some White MMP. Emboss the paste with the quilt embosser and trim to the size of the embosser. Dust sections of the blanket with the range of Pastel Dusts and then brush over the surface with Pearl QFC Lustre Dust. Carefully fold the paste and place on the board edge.

4. Colour small pieces of MMP yellow, pink and green to make the duck, sponge, soap, tissue box and ball. Model some bricks, the talcum powder and baby bottle. Leave to firm before marking with the food pens. Make a small blanket and emboss with a nutmeg grater.

Basket

1. Colour 130g of White MMP with a mixture of Orange and Brown QFC Pastes.

2. Using 80g of the paste, roll an oval shape, flatten the base and bring up the sides with your thumb and finger.

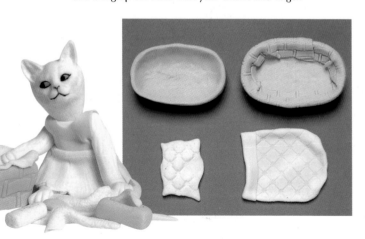

24

3. Roll out the remaining paste and emboss with the basket embosser. Cut to the required length and depth to fit over the base. Fold the paste around the base with the join at the back. Position the finished basket on the cake.

4. Make the pillow from 10g of White MMP. Emboss with the quilt embosser and dust in the same way as for the blanket. Place in the basket.

To Finish

Make the Christening Cats and place in position on top of the cake.

Christening Cats

Make a large and a small head, allow to firm and then paint the eyes green. Paint the mother cat's eyes looking towards her kitten and the little mouse!

Kitten, Bed and Mouse

1. Mould 10g of White MMP into a small cone shape for the body. Push the spaghetti at the neck into the narrow end of the cone and secure with edible glue.

2. Place the kitten in the basket, laying its head on the pillow. You may need to add extra paste under the body to prop it up to the correct height.

3. Emboss and cut out the blanket and dust as before. Fold under the edges and glue into place. Cut out a white strip for the top of the blanket and dust with Pearl QFC Lustre.

4. Model a tiny little mouse in White MMP. Paint with diluted Black QFC

Liquid and Pink QFC Dust. Allow to dry and place on the blanket.

Mother Cat

1. Model the body and legs placing in a sitting position.

2. Cut out a bodice in pink MMP using the template (see page 48).

3. To make the skirt, cut out a pink Garrett frill. Texture the paste using the frilling tool. Pleat the top edge and attach to the body at waist height. (There is no need to make a tail as the dress would hide it.)

4. For the apron, cut out a thin strip of White MMP and wrap it around the waist with the join at the back. Make a bow for the back and secure in place with edible glue. Cut out a portion of the Garrett frill, texture and place in the front of the dress.

5. Model her arms and attach to the body, then position her on the cake. Bend her forward with one arm resting on the basket.

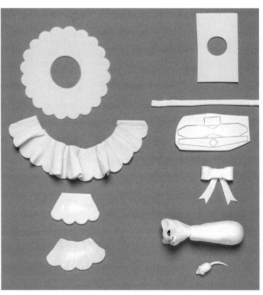

26

Dirty Dealing

Materials

20.5cm/8" square cake

300g/10oz SK Mexican
Modelling Paste (MMP): White

100g/3½oz SK Sugar Florist
Paste (SFP): White

SK QFC Dusts: Brown, Black,
Blue, Dark Green, Orange and
Pink

SK QFC Liquid: Black

SK QFC Lustre Dusts: Gold and
Silver

SK QFC Pastes: Black, Brown,
Dark Green, Green, Orange
and Yellow

SK Hi Strength Paste Food
Colour: Red

SK Magic Sparkle Dust

SK Food Pens: Blackberry,
Daffodil and Poinsettia

Royal icing

Equipment

28cm/11" square cake drum

Bow cutter:
small (JC)

Button tool (HP)

Red ribbon

Method

1. Colour the sugarpaste with Dark Green QFC Paste. Cover the cake and board and place the cake centrally on the board.

2. Place a red ribbon around the base of the cake, securing at the back with royal icing.

Playing Cards

Cut out approximately 26 tiny cards from White SFP. Leave to firm before drawing designs with the food pens.

To Finish

Make the Gangster Cats. Position the cats on the cake and scatter the remaining cards in front of them.

Gangster Cats

Prepare three large cat heads. Cut the left ear off one of the cats – this will be replaced with a hat.

Black and White Cat

1. Colour a small amount of SFP with Brown and Orange QFC Pastes. Make the cigar. Dip the tip in edible glue and then in the Magic Sparkle Dust. Leave to dry.

27

2. Colour 80g of MMP with Brown and Orange QFC Pastes. Use half the paste to make the trousers. Roll a tapered sausage and cut lengthways, then open up the legs and arrange in a seated position.

3. Model the feet from 5g of White MMP and insert into the trousers.

4. Make the body from 10g of White MMP and attach to the top of the trousers.

5. Colour a small amount of SFP with Red Hi Strength Paste Food Colour. Cut out a waistcoat from the template (see page 48). Mark with a stitching wheel. Place in position on the body with the join at the front and attach three red buttons.

6. Make the bow tie from grey coloured SFP and dust with Silver QFC Lustre Dust.

7. Model the arms from 10g of White MMP. Indent the paw with a blade tool and glue the cigar into his left hand. Attach the arms to the body and support the left arm with sponge until dry. Place three of the prepared playing cards under the other paw.

8. Make his tail from 5g of MMP and secure to the cat and cake top.

9. Colour 45g of MMP grey using a little Black QFC Paste. Model the hat from 5g of the grey MMP. Secure the hat to the head with the ear cut off and add a band of brown SFP.

Tabby Cat

1. Make the trousers as before in grey MMP. Add the body and feet.

2. Colour a small amount of SFP with Green

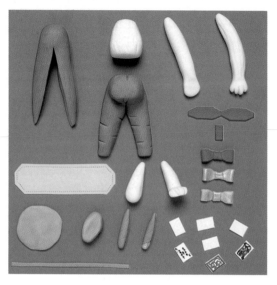

QFC Paste and make the waistcoat. Attach tiny buttons.

3. Make a bow tie from the red SFP.

4. Make the arms as before and bend one arm backwards. Place three Ace cards in his paw and secure with edible glue.

5. Make and attach his tail.

Tortoiseshell Cat

1. Model a large cat in the same way as before, giving him brown trousers.

2. Make a yellow waistcoat and secure to the body. Make a bow tie and dust with Gold QFC Lustre Dust.

3. Make the tail and wrap it around the front of him. Glue an Ace card in the end.

4. Position three cards in his paw and support with sponge until firm.

Painting the Cats

Paint the cats black and white, tabby and tortoiseshell.

Kitties' Night Out

Materials

30.5cm/12" hexagonal cake

1.7kg/3¾lb white sugarpaste

300g/10oz SK Mexican Modelling Paste (MMP): White

60g/2oz SK Sugar Florist Paste (SFP): White

SK QFC Dusts: Black, Blue, Brown, Green, Orange and Pink

SK QFC Liquid: Black

SK QFC Lustre Dust: Silver

SK QFC Pastes: Blue, Brown, Green, Lilac, Orange, Pink and Yellow

SK Hi Strength Paste Food Colour: Black

SK Magic Sparkle Dust

SK Food Pen: Blackberry

SK Silver Dragees: 8mm

SK Dolly Mixtures

Royal icing

Equipment

38cm/15" hexagonal cake drum

Frilling tool (JC)

Garrett frill cutter (OP)

Method

1. Colour the white sugarpaste with Lilac QFC Paste. Cover the board and cake. Place the cake centrally on the board.

2. Secure the Dolly Mixtures and silver dragees around the base of the cake with royal icing.

3. Sprinkle with Magic Sparkle Dust.

4. Roll a piece of MMP and cut out a rectangle for the towel. Texture the paste with a nutmeg grater and place in position on the cake.

30

Hairdryer, Make-up and Bottles

1. Colour a tiny amount of SFP with Hi Strength Black Paste Food Colour. Make the tiny brushes, leads and plugs from the black paste.

2. Colour small amounts of MMP different colours and make all the other items, using the stage work as a guide.

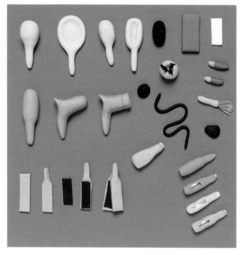

To Finish

Make the Party Girl Cats. Dust their dresses with Magic Sparkle Dust whilst the paste is still soft. Place them on the cake and arrange the various items around them, securing in place with royal icing.

Party Girl Cats

1. Make four medium cat heads and open up the mouth on one.

2. Paint the faces in the usual way. Dust on extra make-up, giving the cats bright eye shadow and blusher. Paint on long eyelashes.

Nicky (Yellow Dress)

1. Model a medium body with 20g of White MMP.

2. Make the legs from 10g of White MMP. Attach to the body in a sitting position.

3. Roll out tiny balls of paste for the bust and glue in place.

4. Cut out a Garrett frill from yellow coloured SFP with the centre cutter missing. Texture with the frilling tool. Cut a cross in the centre.

5. Brush a line of edible glue around the centre of the body and ease the dress into place.

6. Cut out two shoulder straps. Attach under the dress at the front and cross them over at the back.

7. Cut two strips, making them wider at one end, and secure to the front of the dress.

8. Make the arms from 10g of White MMP and secure in place. Place a lipstick in her paw and support until dry.

9. Secure the head to the body with edible glue.

Cally (Green Dress)

1. Make the body and legs as before.

2. Colour some SFP with Green QFC Paste to make the dress. Cut a strip

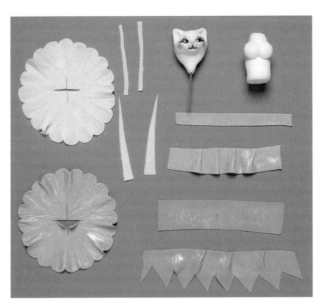

4. Make the arms and place in position, bending her body forward.

5. Secure the head to the body.

Tracy (Pink Dress)

1. Make the body and legs and indent a navel.

2. Make and attach a tail.

3. Colour some SFP with Pink QFC Paste. Cut a strip for the skirt, texture the paste and pleat the top edge. Attach to the body with the join at the back.

4. Cut a very thin pink strip for her top, texture and wrap around the body.

5. Model her arms and glue in position.

6. Secure the head to the body.

Painting the Girls

1. Paint two of the cats as ginger tabbies (see 'Get Well Soon' Cat on page 14). Paint a darker tone for the one holding the fake tan! Using the same technique, paint a grey tabby and a black and white cat.

2. Put some royal icing into a piping bag with a no. 1 nozzle (or snip the tip off the bag). Pipe on the earrings and give Tracy a navel ring. Once the icing is dry, paint with Silver QFC Lustre Dust diluted with clear alcohol.

3. Finally, paint the girls' toes with diluted QFC Dusts.

of paste for the skirt, snip 'V' shapes at the base and texture with a frilling tool. Pleat the top edge and attach to the waist of the body with the join at the back.

3. Cut a thinner strip of paste for the bodice and secure in position with the join at the back. Mark down the front of the bodice with a Dresden tool.

4. Make the tail and attach under the dress.

5. Secure the head to the body.

6. Make the arms and place a bottle of fake tan in her paws.

Amy (Blue Dress)

1. Make the body and legs as before.

2. Colour some SFP with Blue QFC Paste, cut out a Garrett frill and mark a cross in the centre. Texture and glue into place on the body. Mark under the bust line with a blade tool.

3. Model a tail and tuck under the dress.

33

Cat Fight

Materials

20.5cm/8" square cake

1.14kg/2½lb white sugarpaste

200g/7oz Mexican Modelling Paste (MMP): White

100g/3½oz SK Pastillage

SK QFC Dusts: Blue, Brown, Dark Green and Pink

SK QFC Liquid: Black

SK QFC Lustre Dust: Silver

SK QFC Pastes: Blue, Brown, Orange and Yellow

SK Hi Strength Paste Food Colours: Black and Red

Royal icing

Equipment

28cm/11" square cake drum

Plastic cake dowel

Red, white and blue ribbon

Scriber (PME)

Method

1. Cover the board and cake with white sugarpaste. Place the cake centrally on the board.

2. To create a wood effect, mark the sides and board with a scriber.

3. Dilute some Brown QFC Dust with cooled, boiled water or clear alcohol and paint a wash over the marked paste.

Boxing Ring

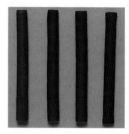

1. For the posts, make up a small amount of pastillage. Colour the pastillage with Black Hi Strength Paste Food Colour. Seal in a food grade polythene bag and leave for approximately two hours for the colour to deepen.

2. Roll the pastillage into cylinders, using a smoother to achieve an even roll. Trim to 9cm length x 1cm width. You will need four but it is advisable to make extras to allow for breakages! Leave to dry on a flat surface in a warm place.

3. Using the end of a dowel, make an indent on each of the four corners of the cake and insert the posts.

4. Tie the three ribbons around the cake with the joins at the back corner.

5. Colour some MMP with Blue QFC Paste for the towel. Roll out the paste, cut out a rectangle and texture the surface using a nutmeg grater. Drape the towel over the back post to hide the joins of the ribbons.

6. Model a bucket from grey coloured MMP and brush with Silver QFC Lustre Dust. Make a sponge in pale blue MMP and place in the bucket.

To Finish

Make the Boxing Cats (see page 36) and place in opposite corners of the boxing ring.

Boxing Cats

1. Prepare two large cat heads.

2. Colour 60g of White MMP with Red Hi Strength Paste Food Colour. Take 40g of the paste for the boxer shorts and roll a tapered sausage. Cut the sausage lengthways down the middle to separate the legs, leaving the top part joined. Bend the legs into a sitting position. Mark creases and open up the ends with a bone tool.

3. Colour 10g of MMP with Yellow QFC Paste. For the waistband, roll a ball of paste, flatten and mark creases. Attach to the shorts. Cut thin strips of yellow and secure them down the sides of the shorts.

4. Model the legs from 5g of White MMP and secure to the shorts.

5. Colour 10g of MMP with Brown and Orange QFC Pastes. Use half this paste to make a pair of boots, following the stage work as a guide. Secure to the legs.

6. Model the top part of the body from 10g of White MMP and attach to the waistband with edible glue.

7. Make the arms from 5g of MMP.

8. Mould the boxing gloves from 5g of the red MMP, using the stage work as a guide. Roll two tiny balls of yellow paste for the cuffs, flatten and mark creases. Attach to the gloves with edible glue.

9. Indent the gloves with a bone tool and attach to the arms.

10. Place the prepared head in position, then bend the arms into place with the boxing gloves up by the cat's mouth. Support well with firm sponge until dry.

11. Place the cat in position on the cake. Model a long tail from 5g of White MMP and wrap it around the post.

12. Make the second cat in the same way, modelling his boxer shorts in dark blue with an orange trim. Position one fist near his face and support well until dry.

13. Place the second cat in position on the cake and make his tail, hanging it over the side of the cake.

14. To finish, pipe laces on their boots with royal icing.

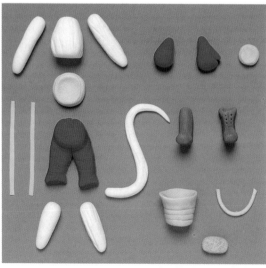

Alley Cats

Materials

20.5cm/8" round cake

910g/2lb white sugarpaste

300g/10oz SK Mexican Modelling Paste (MMP): White

SK QFC Dusts: Black, Brown, Dark Green, Green, Orange, Pink, and Yellow

SK QFC Liquid: Black

SK QFC Lustre Dusts: Gold and Silver

SK QFC Pastes: Blue, Green, Dark Green, Pink and Yellow

SK Magic Sparkle Dust

SK Food Pens: Blackberry and Poinsettia

Royal icing

Equipment

28cm/11" round cake drum

Button tool (HP)

Firm brush/stencil brush

Strip cutter: 7mm (JC)

Yellow ribbon

Method

1. Cover the board and cake with white sugarpaste. Position the cake centrally on the board and leave to firm.

2. Mix some Yellow QFC Dust with Magic Sparkle Dust and dilute with clear alcohol or cooled, boiled water. Stipple the cake and board using a firm brush. Repeat with Green QFC Dust.

3. Place a yellow ribbon around the base of the cake, securing at the back with royal icing.

4. Colour some MMP with Yellow and Green QFC Pastes. Cut out several strips using the cutter, twist into position and place around the base board.

Bottles and Beer Cans

1. Colour 10g of White MMP with Dark Green QFC Paste. Model the bottles using the stage work as a guide. Leave to firm.

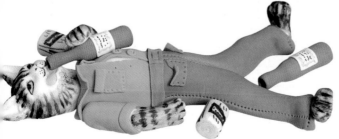

37

2. Make the beer cans and leave to firm.

3. Draw on the bottles and cans with the food pens. Dilute the Gold and Silver QFC Lustre Dusts with cooled, boiled water or clear alcohol and paint the detail onto the labels.

To Finish

Make the Boozy Cats. When the figures are completely dry, place them on the cake and scatter extra bottles and beer cans around them, securing in place with royal icing.

Boozy Cats

1. Prepare three large cat heads, opening their mouths with a Dresden tool.

2. To make the trousers, colour 120g of MMP with Blue QFC Paste. Divide this into three for the three cats.

3. Roll one piece into a tapered sausage and cut lengthways down the middle to separate the legs, leaving the top part joined. Bend into a sitting position and mark creases and stitching. Open up the trouser legs with a bone tool.

4. To make the top of the body, roll 10g of White MMP into a cone shape. Flatten the top and mark the fur. Glue to the trousers and open up the top with a CelStick.

5. Cut out a strip of MMP coloured with Yellow QFC Paste for the shirt and fold over the top edge. Wrap around the body with the join at the front.

6. Model the arms from 10g of MMP. Cut out the sleeves from the yellow paste and wrap them around the arms with the join on the inside edge.

7. Mould the feet from 5g of MMP and glue them into the trousers.

8. Make pockets for the trousers and buttons for the shirt. Secure in place with edible glue.

9. Place the head into position. Make a tiny tongue from pale pink coloured MMP.

10. Bend up one arm and place a bottle in the paw, securing with firm royal icing. Support with pieces of sponge until dry.

11. Repeat the same method for the second sitting cat, giving him a white shirt and placing a beer can in his paw.

12. Make the third cat with a green shirt in a laying down position.

13. Paint the cats in tabby shades (see 'Get Well Soon' Cat on page 14).

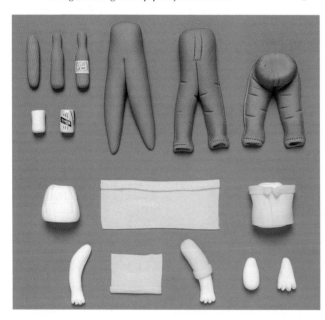

Trick or Treat

Materials

20.5cm/8" hexagonal cake

910g/2lb white sugarpaste

300g/10oz SK Mexican
Modelling Paste (MMP): White

60g/2oz SK Sugar Florist Paste
(SFP): White

SK QFC Dusts: Black, Dark
Green, Orange and Pink

SK QFC Liquid: Black

SK QFC Pastes: Black, Green,
Orange and Red

SK Hi Strength Paste Food
Colour: Black

SK Magic Sparkle Dust

SK Food Pen: Blackberry

Royal icing

Equipment

28cm/11" round cake drum

Circle cutter: 10cm/4"

Oak leaf cutters (OP)

Orange ribbon

Special
Occasion
cutter set
(FMM)

Method

1. Colour 810g of white
sugarpaste with Orange
QFC Paste. Cover the
board and cake and
place the cake centrally
on the board.

2. Colour the remaining
100g of sugarpaste grey
using a little Black QFC
Paste. Roll out the paste
and cut out a 15cm
diameter circle. Place the
circle centrally on the
top of the cake and mark
a crazy paving effect
with a blade tool. Dust
with the Black QFC
Dust.

3. Place a length of orange
ribbon around the base
of the cake and secure
with royal icing.

4. Colour 25g of SFP with
Black Hi Strength Paste
Food Colour. Roll out
and cut out the figures

1. **To Finish step 1** — Cut out the leaves from pale orange SFP. Vein, twist and leave to dry on crinkled foil. Dust the leaves in places with Orange QFC Dust.

2. Position the Halloween Cats on the cake (see opposite).

3. Place the gravestone behind the cats on the cake. Secure with royal icing.

4. Pipe green royal icing around the edge of the paving and scatter leaves onto the icing to hold them in place.

5. Make stones from grey MMP. Place the stones around the leaves and gravestone. Secure a bat to the top of the gravestone with royal icing.

for the side design. You will need six of each and one extra bat for the gravestone. Glue into position around the cake sides with edible glue.

Gravestone

1. Roll out a piece of White MMP to a depth of 1.5cm and cut out a gravestone measuring 5cm x 3cm. Mark indents down the front. Make a small piece for the top, slightly smaller in width and rounded. Secure to the bottom part with edible glue and leave to firm.

2. Dust the gravestone with Black QFC Dust. Mark the inscription with a Blackberry Food Pen.

Cauldron

Roll a 10g ball of black MMP and indent the top with a bone tool. Glue a handle to the front. Make tiny sweets from red, orange and green MMP and place these in the cauldron. Dust with the Magic Sparkle Dust. Make a tiny little mouse, dust and place on the sweets.

Halloween Cats

1. Colour 60g of MMP with Black Hi Strength Paste Food Colour. Make a large and a small cat head. Leave to firm.

2. Dust the eyes dark green and the cheeks and ears pink. Paint the pupils with Black QFC Liquid.

Pumpkin Cat

1. For the pumpkin body, colour 100g of White MMP with Orange QFC Paste. Roll into a ball and mark lines down the pumpkin to form segments. Mark the face indents with a Dresden tool, then glue in tiny pieces of black paste cut to shape.

2. Model a small ball of green paste for the top, indent and glue in position.

3. Twist a large CelStick into the top and push the large cat head into position. Make a small pumpkin hat and secure on top of the head with edible glue.

4. Position the cat on the cake, then make the arms, legs and tail from 25g of black MMP and glue in place.

Little Ghost Cat

1. Mould a cone from 5g of White MMP. For the cloak, roll out some more white paste and cut out a 10cm circle, ensuring it is large enough to drape over the cone.

2. Model the arms from small cones of paste, mark creases and indent the wide end.

3. Make tiny little paws from black paste and attach to the arms.

4. Open up the top of the body and position the head.

5. Make a pointed hat from White MMP, using the stage work as a guide. Place on the cat's head when firm.

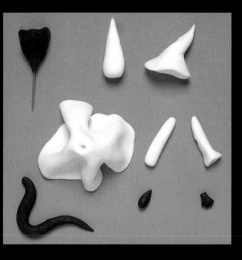

Christmas Catastrophe!

Materials

20.5cm/8" round cake

1.14kg/2½lb white sugarpaste

300g/10oz SK Mexican Modelling Paste (MMP): White

100g/3½oz SK Pastillage

60g/2oz SK Sugar Florist Paste (SFP): White

SK QFC Dusts: Blue, Green, Pink and Red

SK QFC Lustre Dust: Silver

SK QFC Liquid: Black

SK QFC Pastes: Brown, Green, Red and Yellow

SK Hi Strength Paste Food Colour: Red

SK Food Pens: Holly/Ivy and Poinsettia

Caster sugar

Equipment

33cm/13" round cake drum

Circle cutter: 4cm/1¾"

Frilling tool (JC)

Garrett frill cutter (OP)

Method

1. Cover the board with white sugarpaste and leave to firm. Dilute some Red QFC Dust with clear alcohol or cooled, boiled water and stipple around the outside edge of the board.

2. Cover the cake with a very thin layer of white sugarpaste. Place on the board towards the back.

3. For the tablecloth, cut out a 33cm diameter circle of white sugarpaste and drape over the cake. Place the tablecloth towards the front as if the naughty cats are pulling it off!

Plates, Food and Crackers

1. Roll out some pastillage and cut out several plates using the medium-sized centre cutter of the Garrett frill set. Indent an inner circle using the

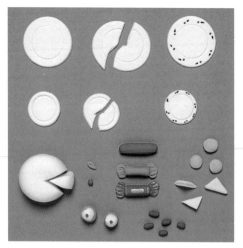

Christmas Cats

Make four medium cat heads. Open the mouths of two cats. Give them blue eyes and pink cheeks.

small centre cutter. Make several larger plates in the same way using a 4cm circle cutter and indent with the medium Garrett frill centre cutter. Cut some of the plates into uneven pieces for the broken ones. Leave to firm before decorating with Holly/Ivy and Poinsettia Food Pens.

2. Make all the food from coloured MMP. Brush the mince pies with edible glue and sprinkle with caster sugar.

3. Make several crackers and paint with Silver QFC Lustre Dust mixed with clear alcohol or cooled, boiled water.

To Finish

1. Make the Christmas Cats and arrange on the cake before they have dried so that they can be moved into position.

2. Place all the plates, food and crackers around the cats, securing with royal icing.

The Boys

1. For the trousers on the first boy cat, roll a tapered sausage from 10g of green MMP. Cut and shape the legs. Mark creases and open up the trouser ends.

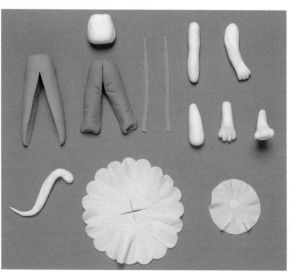

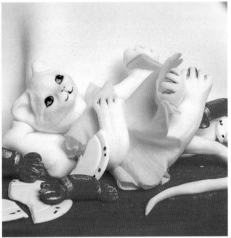

2. Make the feet from 5g of White MMP and glue in place.

3. Model the top of the body from 5g of White MMP.

4. Cut two straps from green paste, drape them over the shoulders and cut to size. Indent at the waist with a small CelStick.

5. Model the arms from 5g of White MMP.

6. Attach the head and position the cat on the side of the cake. Bend the arms upwards so the cat looks as if he is hanging onto the tablecloth.

7. Model a tail and curl into place.

8. Repeat this method for the second boy, giving him orange trousers. Add a tiny pink tongue in his mouth.

The Girls

1. To make the girl in the red dress, model the body from 20g of White MMP.

2. Make the legs from 5g of White MMP and secure to the

body so that the cat is leaning forward.

3. Colour 25g of White SFP with Red Hi Strength Paste Food Colour and roll out thinly. Cut out a Garrett frill with the centre cutter missing and texture using the frilling tool. Cut a cross in the centre and glue in place over the body.

4. Make and attach the tail.

5. Model the arms from 5g of White MMP and secure in place.

6. Cut out a 4cm diameter circle for the collar and texture with a frilling tool. Place in position.

7. Glue a mince pie in the cat's mouth and attach her head.

8. Place the cat on top of the cake and bend forward into a crouched position.

9. Make the second girl cat in a similar way with a yellow dress. Bend the legs up and position the cat on her back. Glue a sandwich in her hand.

47

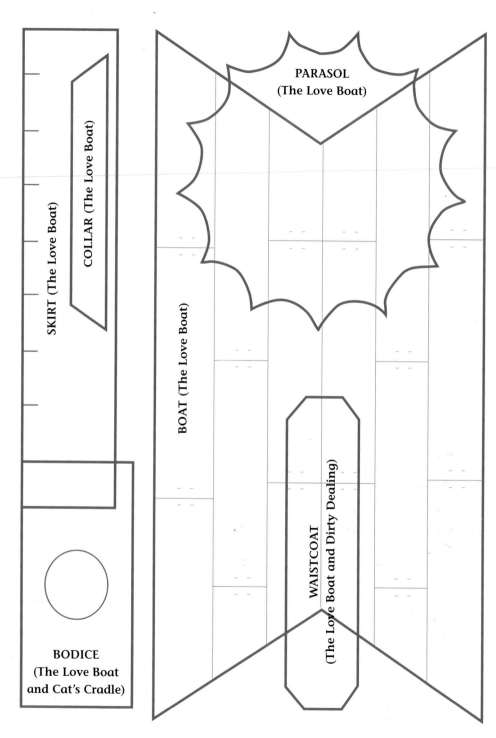

SKIRT (The Love Boat)

COLLAR (The Love Boat)

BODICE
(The Love Boat
and Cat's Cradle)

BOAT (The Love Boat)

PARASOL
(The Love Boat)

WAISTCOAT
(The Love Boat and Dirty Dealing)